# THE
# Hoover Dam

BY LUKE GABRIEL

Published by The Child's World®
1980 Lookout Drive • Mankato, MN 56003-1705
800-599-READ • www.childsworld.com

Acknowledgments
The Child's World®: Mary Berendes, Publishing Director
The Design Lab: Design
Jody Jensen Shaffer; Editing
Red Line Editorial: Photo Research

Photo credits
Shutterstock Images, cover; Brand X Pictures, 5; Popperfoto/
Getty Images, 6, 9; United States Bureau of Reclamation/Library
of Congress, 10; Harris & Ewing/Library of Congress, 13; AP
Images, 14; Library of Congress, 17; Keith Bell/Shutterstock
Images, 18; Creatas, 21

ISBN 9781623239565
LCCN 2013947391

Printed in the United States of America
Mankato, MN
November, 2013
PA02189

## ABOUT THE AUTHOR

*Luke Gabriel enjoys traveling, reading, playing games with his wife, and wrestling with his five children. He and his family live in Eagan, Minnesota.*

# TABLE OF CONTENTS

# The Colorado River

"Look out! Flood!" These were the cries of the farmers in the Imperial Valley in California. The year was 1905. Huge rainstorms had caused the Colorado River to overflow. It flooded miles of farms, railroads, and buildings. In 1916, the river flooded again, this time damaging California's Yuma Valley. Many people moved away forever. For people still living near the river, life was hard.

In 1918, an **engineer** named Arthur P. Davis recommended building a huge **concrete** dam to control the river and save homes and farmland. He thought an area called Boulder Canyon was the best place—where the river separates the states of Arizona and Nevada. In 1928, Congress approved Davis's plan.

*This part of the Colorado River is called Horseshoe Bend.*

*This photo shows the catwalks used by workers on the Hoover Dam.*

# Preparing to Build

BOOM! BOOM! In 1931, the sound of explosions could be heard from miles away. Workers were putting dynamite into the walls of Boulder Canyon on both sides of the Colorado River. They were digging four huge tunnels to **divert** the river so the dam could be built.

Building the tunnels was not easy. At first, there were no roads into the Boulder Canyon area. Equipment, supplies, and workers had to be carried in by boat. Workers crossed the river on dangerous small bridges called **catwalks**. The catwalks were held up by steel cables. Cold winds blew through the canyon during the winter, dropping the temperature to near freezing. During the summer, the hot sun raised the temperature to over 120 degrees (49 C). But through it all, the tunnels had to be built.

# Building the Tunnels

It took about ten months to dig the tunnels. Workers used 2,000 pounds (907 kilograms) of dynamite for every 14 feet (4 meters). The tunnels were 56 feet (17 meters) wide and had a combined length of more than three miles (almost five kilometers).

The next step was to make the tunnels strong and watertight. It took another eight months to line the tunnels with concrete. Train tracks were laid down in the tunnels so workers could move giant cranes through. The cranes helped workers frame the tunnels with steel and line the walls with concrete. When finished, the tunnels' concrete linings were three feet (1 meter) thick.

At the end of 1932, the tunnels were ready. Workers blocked the river by dumping tons of rocks into it. The water rose up and flowed into the tunnels, creating a big dry spot in the bottom of Boulder Canyon. Now the dam could be built!

*A lot of dynamite was used in building Hoover Dam.*

*This high-scaler is using a special air-pressure hammer.*

# The High-Scalers

"Look out below!" That was what a **high-scaler** would yell if rocks were falling. High-scalers were workers who used ropes to climb down the walls and cliffs of Boulder Canyon. Their job was to use dynamite, jackhammers, and other tools to clear away loose rock. They would also carry tools and other workers to places in the canyon that couldn't be reached any other way.

Being a high-scaler was dangerous. Many high-scalers were hurt or killed by falling rocks and tools. Some even fell into the canyon. To make their job safer, they invented their own hard hats. They used these hard hats until real hard hats could be brought in for them to use.

# Mixing Concrete

Where did the workers get all the concrete for lining the tunnels and building the dam? They made it themselves. Concrete is made of sand, water, cement, and crushed rock. Sand and water were easy to find, and cement could be brought in on trucks. But what about the crushed rock?

It took several months, but workers found a giant layer of rocks in Arizona six miles (about 10 kilometers) away from the dam site. Workers scooped the rocks onto trains and hauled them to the work site. The rocks were separated by size. Any rock over nine inches had to be crushed. The proper-sized rocks were then loaded onto other trains and hauled to the concrete mixing plant.

*This picture shows the dam under construction.*

*This is how Boulder City looked in its early days.*

# Boulder City

As the months went by, more and more workers were needed to build the dam. The new workers had no place to live, so houses and a big dining hall were built. The dining hall could serve 6,000 meals every day. Every week the dining hall used about 60,000 eggs, 10,000 pounds (4,536 kilograms) of meat, and 24,000 pounds (10,886 kilograms) of fruits and vegetables. The workers and their families were hungry!

This growing town was named Boulder City. Although it wasn't fancy, Boulder City provided a nearby place for workers to live. It had no trees, and it was very hot and dry. As more and more people moved in, schoolhouses, a hospital, a library, and a church were built.

# Building the Dam

Concrete for the dam was poured between 1933 and 1935. Cranes lifted the concrete in giant dump buckets. Once a bucket was lifted to the right spot, the bottom opened and the concrete poured out. A crew of workers called **puddlers** used shovels to quickly smooth out the concrete.

The concrete then had to set and harden. To help it set faster, the concrete was poured in small sections. After the concrete hardened, a mixture of cement and water called **grout** was then squeezed into any cracks that were found. This made the entire dam watertight.

When finished, the dam was 726 feet (221 meters) tall. At the top it was 1,244 feet (379 meters) long and 45 feet (about 14 meters) wide. The dam was curved to make it stronger. The dam weighed more than 13 billion pounds (almost 6 billion kilograms)!

This crane is handling a dump bucket for pouring out concrete.

*These are the huge turbines in the dam's power plant.*

# Making Electricity

Seventeen big machines called **turbines** were installed in the power plant section of the dam. Water flowing through the dam turned the turbines, producing electricity. This way of making electricity is called **hydroelectric power**. The electricity was sold to electric companies that provided power to 1.3 million people in Nevada, Arizona, and California. The money from the electricity was more than enough to cover the entire cost of building the dam!

The water behind the dam is called a **reservoir**. This reservoir is named Lake Mead. Lake Mead is almost 500 feet (152 meters) deep in some places. It is 120 miles (193 kilometers) long. Each year, more than 9 million people visit Lake Mead to swim, boat, and fish.

# Naming the Dam

In September of 1935, President Franklin Roosevelt visited the opening of the dam. The dam had been called Boulder Dam for many years. Some people suggested that the dam should be named after President Herbert Hoover. They suggested this because most of the work on the dam was completed while Hoover was president. In April of 1947, President Harry Truman renamed the dam Hoover Dam. That's the name it still has today.

Thousands of people visit Hoover Dam every year. There you can take a tour of the inside and walk across the top of the dam. Visitors can see the turbines and the tunnels, too. If you're near the Colorado River or Las Vegas, Nevada, don't forget to visit Hoover Dam!

*Here you can see Lake Mead behind Hoover Dam.*

# Glossary

**catwalks (KAT-walks)** Catwalks are small bridges hung in the air. Catwalks were used by the workers building Hoover Dam.

**concrete (KON-kreet)** Concrete is a mixture of sand, water, and cement. The Hoover Dam is made of concrete.

**divert (dy-VERT)** To divert a river means to change where the water flows. To build Hoover Dam, the Colorado River had to be diverted by tunnels.

**engineer (en-jin-EER)** An engineer is a person who designs and plans structures or machines. Arthur P. Davis was an engineer.

**grout (GROWT)** Grout is a cement and water mixture used to plug up cracks. Grout was used to plug up the cracks of Hoover Dam.

**high-scaler (HY-skay-ler)** High-scalers were workers who hung from ropes to clear away loose rock from canyon walls. Many high-scalers helped to build Hoover Dam.

**hydroelectric power (hy-dro-ee-LEK-trik POW-er)** Hydroelectric power is electricity produced by water flowing through a dam. Hoover Dam is a large producer of hydroelectric power.

**puddlers (PUD-lerz)** A puddler was a type of concrete worker who smoothed wet concrete. Many puddlers helped pour the concrete of Hoover Dam.

**reservoir (REZ-ur-vwar)** A reservoir is a lake created by damming up a river. Hoover Dam created the largest reservoir in the United States. It is called Lake Mead.

**turbines (TUR-bynz)** Turbines are engines inside a dam that make hydroelectric power. The Hoover Dam has 17 main turbines.

# Find Out More

## IN THE LIBRARY

Graham, Ian, and David Antram (illustrator). *You Wouldn't Want to Work on the Hoover Dam!* New York: Franklin Watts, 2012.

Mann, Elizabeth, and Alan Witschonke (illustrator). *The Hoover Dam: The Story of Hard Times, Tough People and The Taming of a Wild River.* New York: Mikaya, 2006.

Miller, Heather. *The Hoover Dam.* Chicago: Norwood House Press, 2013.

Zuehlke, Jeffrey. *The Hoover Dam.* Minneapolis, MN: Lerner, 2010.

## ON THE WEB

Visit our Web site for lots of links about the Hoover Dam:
*www.childsworld.com/links*

Note to Parents, Teachers, and Librarians: We routinely check our Web links to make sure they're safe, active sites—so encourage your readers to check them out!

# Index